Introducing
SEED COLLAGE

CARYL AND GORDON SIMMS

B T Batsford Limited   *London*

Watson-Guptill Publications   *New York*

© *Caryl and Gordon Simms 1971*
First published 1971
Reprinted 1972
ISBN 0 7134 2428 1
Watson-Guptill ISBN 0-8230-6315-1
Library of Congress Catalog Card Number 75-114199

Filmset in 11 on 12½ point Monotype Century Medium
by Filmtype Services Limited, Scarborough
Printed and bound in Denmark by
F E Bording Limited, Copenhagen
for the Publishers
B T Batsford Limited
4 Fitzhardinge Street, London W 1
and
Watson-Guptill Publications
165 West 46 Street, New York, NY 10036

Contents

Acknowledgment

We would like to express our gratitude to all who have so willingly contributed work to this book; and to Carmel Cauchi for taking the photographs, for drawing figures 63 to 65, 71 to 74, 82 to 83, and for his encouragement and invaluable advice.

C. and G.S.
1971

Figures 55 and 96 are based on illustrations from Fontana Unesco Art Books publication *Aboriginal Paintings* by Charles P. Mountford, pages 20 and 24
Figure 89 is based on an illustration from Fontana Unesco Art Books publication *Bhuddist Paintings* by D. B. Dhanapala, page 28
Figure 93 is based on an illustration from Fontana Unesco Art Books publication *Mexican Wall-Paintings* by Ignacio Bernal, page 4

Introduction

For the purposes of this book 'seeds' is a term embracing beans, peas, lentils and grain as well as the seeds of fruit and flowers. Although seeds have been used with other materials in collage, the emphasis here is on exploiting seeds in their natural state, for it is part of the enjoyment of this work that the seed, itself visually unexciting, can be used to create pictures which are satisfying, beautiful and fun to make.

For those who do not have the convenience of a college or school to provide materials, it may be welcome to learn that here is a genuine 'do-it-yourself' medium. All the seeds mentioned in this book, and no doubt a good many more that the reader may discover for himself, are easily obtainable from shops or, of course, the plants and fruits themselves. Moreover, they can be bought for quite small sums, yet in large quantities. Equally, the other equipment needed to actually construct a permanent picture (though this may not be required merely as a matter of course) is cheap and accessible. We hope that anyone who is curious to experiment for himself will find in this book the general advice and practical tips that will anticipate the few problems which exist, and perhaps stimulation to create work which he enjoys and finds rewarding.

For the art teacher or student teacher there is a special chapter, covering the entire age range, on the use of this medium in schools. Children find this work exciting and can very soon acquire the necessary techniques. This is confirmed by the illustrations in chapter four, all of which show children's first attempts. Naturally the methods of introduction will vary, but the guiding principles here may assist the development of this work into something educationally and aesthetically satisfying.

Finally, we hope that the art student looking for new ideas may find this book of some value. Seeds can be used to produce fascinating collages either with other materials or by themselves. The immense variety in seeds allows scope for technical experiment; yet at the same time the limitations of the medium impose restrictions and disciplines that are probably more strict than in any other form of collage.

One   The seeds

This chapter deals with a representative selection of each seed type rather than a duplication of seeds which are very similar to each other. A comprehensive list of the seeds we have found to date, together with their main features, may be found on page 102.

The seeds in the following illustrations do not necessarily fall into family groups, but have been arranged according to shape and size. For this reason figures 2 to 16 are reproduced to actual size. However, it should be noted that in nearly all types of seed there is variation in colour, while in many, differences in the markings occur. We have indicated where either of these features differ substantially, particularly in cases where we think it worthwhile to sort through the seeds to separate them into categories. Variations of this kind are especially noticeable when seeds from different consignments are compared.

Dwarf french (kidney) bean, butter (lima) bean, rose coco (cacao) bean, black-eye bean
The coat of the smooth, shiny dwarf french bean may vary from pale crimson to black. It is almost identical in size to the rose coco bean, which is pinky-brown with darker brown speckles. Careful selection of the rose coco beans will usually reveal a small quantity which lack

2 Dwarf french (kidney) bean, butter (lima) bean, rose coco (cacao) bean, black-eye bean

markings or on which the markings are very subdued, the colours of these ranging from beige to khaki. Larger and flatter is the butter bean. Its smooth, cream coat tends to discolour when varnished as, like most other 'white' seeds, it absorbs a certain amount of varnish. This tendency can be overcome by rubbing the seed lightly with a rag dipped in very little varnish instead of applying the normal brushing process. (See page 36.)

The black-eye bean lacks the normal bean characteristic of a smooth, shiny skin. Here the cream coat is wrinkled and papery, and each bean has a black patch round the radicle.

All these beans may be used either way up as the sides are similar in shape. However, the curve of the beans lends itself for use in consistently curving lines or areas. The black-eye beans can be arranged with striking effect if placed with their black patches uppermost, but more adhesive is then needed to secure them.

12

3   Maple pea, haricot bean, tickbean, dried pea

Maple pea, haricot bean, tickbean, dried pea
All the beans and peas here have a smooth and fairly shiny skin, and all
are almost spherical. They are extremely appropriate for outlining and
infilling large areas as they are compact and provide interesting texture. The tickbean ranges from mid- to dark brown and the speckled
maple pea from mid- to light brown; these two are often bought together
as pigeon peas, but can easily be sorted and separated. The slightly
waxy coat of the tickbean requires more adhesive than most seeds.
The haricot bean is white and the dried pea a very light green.

13

4   Split pea, continental lentil, red lentil

Split pea, continental lentil, red lentil
Both the gold split pea and the red lentil (which in fact tends towards orange) are only single halves of the original seeds, consequently having one flat and one convex side. They are equally effective whether scattered haphazardly or placed individually.

The continental lentil ranges from light green, through khaki to brown. It retains its covering to present two similar sides, but if the skin is opened pale yellow halves are revealed. This lentil, being almost flat, affords good background cover in larger pictures.

15

5 Pumpkin seed   6 Coffee bean

Pumpkin seed
The radicles of these flat, oval seeds protrude at one end. The colour of an individual seed may vary, and the entire colour range is from an olive to an extremely pale green.

Coffee bean
One side of this bean is flat with a slit running the length of it, the other is rounded. Oval and smooth, the usually rich dark brown bean provides one of the deepest tones available.

7   Chick pea

Chick pea
A pinky beige shade, the round, knobbly appearance of the chick pea –
similar indeed to a trussed chicken – provides a useful contrast to the
more regular seeds.

17

8   Polished rice, patna (long-grained) rice, pearl barley, wheat

Polished rice, patna (long-grained) rice, pearl barley, wheat
Both types of rice present interesting tones when placed on a coloured
ground because they are translucent. The patna (or long-grained)
variety is yellowish, thin and flat, whereas the polished rice is whiter
and more rounded.

Pearl barley is similar in shape and size to polished rice, but is much
more opaque. One face has a slit running the entire length, a character-
istic shared by wheat, which is larger than pearl barley and a golden
brown in colour.

9　Maize (Indian corn)

Maize (Indian corn)
The golden-yellow, semi-translucent kernels are irregular in both
shape and size. Surrounding the radicle is an area of opaque beige skin.
Because it is much flatter than most seeds, maize appears to sparkle
when varnished.

19

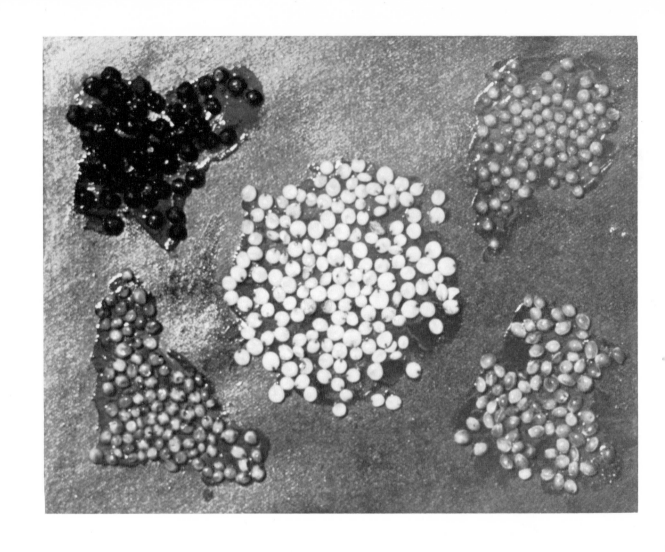

10   Black peppercorn, milo, white dari, white peppercorn, hemp

11   Plum stone

Black peppercorn, milo, white dari, white peppercorn, hemp
The black peppercorn is vastly different from its white counterpart: its
colouring is mid-brown to black – as opposed to beige to light brown; it
is much larger and its skin is wrinkled into craters instead of being
evenly divided by ridges. Milo, when varnished – a process which en-
hances it greatly – produces varying shades of orange. This round seed
has a slight flattening on one side. The larger and flatter white dari has
a black radicle surrounded by a tinge of yellow.
   The delicately veined skin of hemp is smooth and greenish-grey.

Plum stone
These stones are well worth the effort of collecting as their size makes a
bold visual impression.

12 Sunflower seed

Sunflower seed
Because of the many colours and markings to be found these are amongst the most fascinating seeds of all. A complete colour range from white, through silver grey, beige, brown to black is obtainable from most packets. The degree to which the markings vary is also extensive, and one seed alone may suggest quite complicated designs such as to be found on feathers or fur. Strong directional values can be achieved with these seeds, which are often worth sorting to create tonal areas.

22

13 Grass seed, mustard seed, teazle, maw (poppy seed), niger (rantil), red rape seed, linseed, plate millet (hay seed), mazagan canary seed

Grass seed, mustard seed, teazle, maw (poppy seed),
Niger (rantil), red rape seed, linseed, plate millet (hay seed),
mazagan canary seed
These and several others like them (whole cummin seed, black rape seed, etc.) are probably most useful for scattering for background or in small detailed areas, as they are too tiny for individual placing. They can also be used for mixing with other seeds to make slightly lighter or darker tones. The wide tonal range seen here includes maw, the only small blue seed we have found to date.

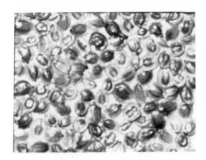

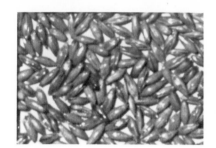

14 *Above left* Parsnip
15 *Below left* Clipped oat
16 *Right* Gunga bean

Parsnip seed
From garden or seed packet can be obtained one of the most beautiful seeds. These flat, ochre to brown seeds with dark brown lines are papery and delicate, giving a valuable texture contrast when used with plain, rounded seeds.

Clipped oat
Similar in form to wheat, oats are longer, thinner and paler.

Gunga bean
Generally speckled, these smooth, roundish beans may each include beige, mid- and dark brown markings. Some, at either extreme of the colour range, are almost unmarked, making the gunga bean yet another variety which is worth sorting.

Two   *First experiments*

Before attempting to make a picture it is most important to experiment with the seeds, seeing how many shapes can be made with one seed type. These shapes may suggest many ideas, and more may be evoked by using next a limited number of seed types in simple patterns. These early ventures need take up very little time, as it is obviously sufficient to arrange the seeds loosely on a board.

Many of the illustrations in this chapter use seeds already described. Figure 17 (employing the same combination of seeds as figure 3) and figure 18 both use a straightforward pattern of repeated rows. The selection of light and dark pumpkin seeds (figure 19) used alternately begins to add a dimensional quality.

Repetition is taken a stage further in the key pattern (figure 20) where the cowpeas and pale gunga beans yield a softer interpretation of the traditional design. Despite their rounded quality seeds readily adapt to the restrictions imposed by angles and straight lines. This is demonstrated in figure 21, an exercise based on triangles, but again some edges have been deliberately softened to make a less harsh impact.

The beans in the flamboyant figure 22 were allowed to follow their natural curves, while in the centre a selection of lighter and darker dwarf french beans was made. Figure 23 develops the use of curves as

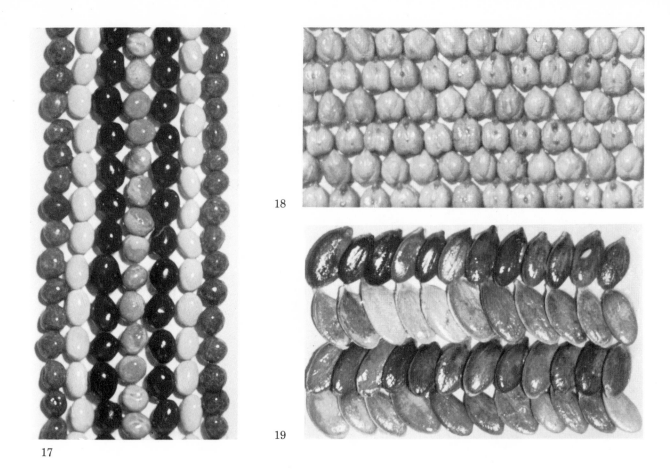

17

18

19

the exercises gradually evolve to circular shapes. The sunflower seeds of figure 25 also demonstrate the use of one seed type to make a tonal study. The sample sheet of circles, employing many seed types (figure 26) indicates something of the versatility of the medium, while figure 27 (see also Plate 1) shows a completed picture based on circular moulds which had formed on home-made wine.

20

21

27

22

23

PLATE 1 *Growth* 305 mm × 305 mm (12 in. × 12 in.)
Picture based on circular moulds which had formed on home-made wine

24   Detail from *Microbe*   457 mm × 610 mm (18 in × 24 in.) by Linda Farrar

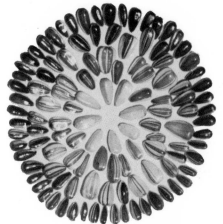

25

26

27 *Growth* 305 mm × 305 mm (12 in. × 12 in.) (see also Plate 1)

Three   Design and picture construction

Design is the essential stage in preparing any satisfactory picture, and in this medium there must be many considerations before construction of the picture begins. The most important questions concern the versatility and limitations of seeds. Whereas with the brush one stroke may create a fine distinction or hint of a shadow, with seeds any such effect has to be planned – seeds are rigid and unchanging, and adhesives dry more quickly than paint. Of course ideas may be developed or areas rearranged as the picture progresses (there is a drying time with most adhesives which allows for second thoughts) but a good concept of what is to be attempted in the picture is vital before work begins.

Selection of subject
Selection of the subject leads to the crucial theme of what is worth doing in seeds that other media may not achieve as well. Obviously any kind of picture can be made with seeds but, apart from experimenting with this form for the experience alone, there is little point in gaining only moderate satisfaction from a partially successful picture which would have been better undertaken in another medium. This is where early experiments are invaluable. Once a feeling for the materials develops from simple, temporary arrangements as in chapter two, an

understanding of how they can effectively be used for making pictures will unfold and appropriate subjects suggest themselves (here the chapter on subject sources may be of assistance).

When a subject has been chosen it may be necessary to substitute colour, as the exact tones required may not be available, but any other adaptations will probably be made automatically. For instance, simplification of the subject is often desirable in order to avoid overworking an area and to guarantee a clear impression. An example of this occurs in figure 100 where the complicated markings of tawny owls are amply suggested rather than faithfully copied. Such modification as this presents a challenge which makes the work extremely interesting.

Next, the size of the picture must be decided, and here it is important to remember that background, if used, should never be merely a vague area surrounding the subject, but always an integral part of it – the background must complement the subject, not detract from it by being out of proportion or ill-suited in colour or texture. Figures 27 (see also Plate 1) and 105 illustrate use of a raised background to recess the subject, while backgrounds which are as interesting in shape as the subjects can be found in figures 89, 92 and 93.

Transfer of design
The design can now be drawn on to the board. If working from a sketch, a quick way of ensuring that the proportions of the drawing are accurately preserved in the picture is to divide both sketch and board with ruled pencil lines into quarters. It is then relatively easy to copy the detail from each section, and further sub-division can be made if necessitated by the subject-matter. This process can be used for making any size picture from any size sketch.

Selection of seeds
It is advisable to limit the seed selection for a picture in order to achieve fluidity and bold design. We have found it helpful when planning a picture to group handfuls of the selected seeds alongside each other to ensure that they provide the desired relationship.

The choice of seeds will of course be determined by which types have been made available. Here it is well to bear in mind the sources from

33

which seeds may be obtained. There are those which may be extracted from fruit and flowers in the home and garden, but any pips or seeds need to be thoroughly dry before use in a picture, otherwise mould or discoloration could occur even after the application of varnish. It might be thought tedious to collect small amounts of seeds or pips at a time, but sufficient number to work a small area can accrue very quickly.

A wide variety of seeds can be bought in supermarkets, grocery stores, continental, gourmet and pet shops. It is worth checking that the seeds appear to be clean and unbroken – unless they are in sealed packets. Try to decide in advance how many seeds of each type will be needed, remembering that a packet of small seeds will probably serve several pictures and that if the seeds are in bins an ounce is as easy to buy as a pound. On the other hand avoid underestimating the quantities required so that each seed type can be obtained from the same source. This is most important for, as we have already observed, seeds in separate consignments often differ in size or colour.

Making the base
Next a base is needed on which to place the seeds. We think insulating board is the most satisfactory. Its main advantages are that it can easily be cut to any shape or size with a small saw, and that it is soft enough to absorb shock (it is 13 mm ($\frac{1}{2}$ in.) thick); yet usually it is hard enough not to flake at the edges or warp – though this could happen if it were stacked at an angle for a long time. Moreover, it is very light to hang or carry, even when framed.

Insulating board provides a ready-made natural ground, but should a painted ground be desired it is worth noting that many types of paint are too easily absorbed to be of any use. However, an acrylic or co-polymer emulsion has proved very successful. There is a wide range of colours available, and these can be mixed to give further choice. Such paint, in keeping with the seeds, appears glossy under varnish.

There are many makes of insulating board obtainable from do-it-yourself shops, timber merchants or lumber yards. The most suitable is one which yields a little to pressure from the thumb yet is firm enough to retain its surface texture. Other points to observe when buying are that the corners have not been damaged by poor storage and that the compressed layers which make up the board are firm – if they are flaking, or too far apart, framing will be difficult. Suppliers often offer to cut this board into transportable sizes, and many retailers are prepared to sell very small pieces.

For experimental work cardboard and hardboard are quite adequate but, apart from being lightweight, do not share the advantages of insulating board. Furthermore, such bases tend to become very dark when varnished. Most of the illustrations for chapters one, two and four were carried out on cardboard or thick paper.

The adhesive which we have found most satisfactory is *Dufix* (a British glue), which is useful not only for sticking down seeds and assisting with frames, but also for other types of collage such as paper and fabric. A spatula is provided with this brand, which has the important characteristic of drying absolutely transparently, so that any adhesive accidentally left on the tops of the seeds does not show. *Evostick Resin 'W'* (another British glue) is also suitable for seed collage, and both brands are obtainable in small, cheap quantities if desired. The US equivalents of these British glues are *Elmer's* glue and *Sobo*.

Working the picture

When working the picture it is best to cover only a small area of the board at a time, spreading the adhesive fairly thickly. There is a drying time in which the seeds can be placed (or rearranged if necessary) and during which the adhesive is quite pliable. Once dry, the adhesive affords a strong bond. The polythene spatula is used to spread the adhesive into which the point of a pencil can be dipped to pick up the individual seeds. This is time-saving and more convenient than fumbling with the fingers.

Once the picture is complete it is advisable to varnish it for several reasons. Varnishing protects the picture from damp and dust, provides a firmer bond between adjacent seeds and prevents fading. Additionally, all seeds are enhanced by a coat of varnish. Assuming that a clear varnish is required, polyurethane, though relatively expensive, is to be recommended for its resilience. We have found *Permshine* (a British polyurethane varnish) well-suited to the task, as yellowing is minimal. Boat-builder's varnishes which require two components to be mixed and used immediately are equally effective but unduly laborious for small-scale work of this nature. Colourless nail polish is ideal, but because of its price cannot be recommended for large-scale application. Up to three coats of clear polyurethane will enrich but not alter the colour of the seeds. More than three coats will provide a slightly 'tanned' glaze which may look attractive on the right picture. *Valspar* extra pale varnish is inexpensive and satisfactory, but does not have the same sealing power as polyurethane. However, *Valspar* also produce a selection of wood-stain varnishes which provide interesting effects.

Before application of the varnish, make sure that there are no loose seeds (unless they are strays which, if in difficult positions, can be removed by vacuum cleaner, feather duster or pin). Apply the varnish with a 25 mm to 50 mm (1 in. to 2 in.) brush, making sure that the bristles coat the sides of the seeds as well as the tops. All white seeds tend to become discoloured as they absorb the varnish. While this character-istic may be exploited to create interesting irregularities, it can be overcome by brushing or wiping with a cloth as thin a coat as possible over the susceptible seeds.

Framing the picture
The final stage of making the picture is that of framing. It is important to leave this process until the varnish is dry, otherwise the vibrations caused by hammering could loosen the seeds. As glass is likely to reflect light and is anyway rendered unnecessary by the protection of the varnish, making the frame can be a reasonably straightforward process.

The wood used to frame the picture should be wide enough to project beyond the largest seeds in order to give extra protection from dust. Staff beading, about 22 mm ($\frac{7}{8}$ in.) thick, is suitable for smaller seeds and, with its rounded edge, is sympathetic to the medium. For pictures with bigger seeds we have used 19 mm × 38 mm ($\frac{3}{4}$ in. × $1\frac{1}{2}$ in.) deal (a cheap wood, and one that lends itself to seed pictures by virtue of its natural, grained appearance). Obviously individual taste will influence the choice of framing material, for the actual appearance of the frame may add considerably to the final effect of the picture. Similarly, a decision has to be made concerning the finish of the frame. Any treat-ment of the wood should be given before the frame is put on.

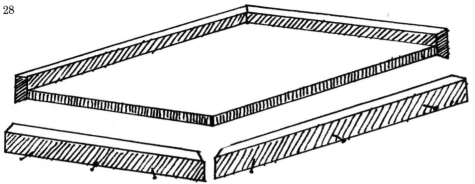

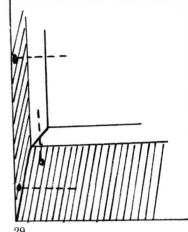

A simple framing method is given below. Once the wood has been chosen, all that is needed is a cheap mitre block (known in the USA as a miter box) to ensure neat corners, a hammer, some panel pins (brads) and adhesive:

(a) Cut and mitre each piece so that inside edge matches respective side of picture (figure 28).

(b) Hammer panel pins partway into each piece at about 152 mm (6 in.) intervals, leaving 50 mm to 75 mm (2 in. to 3 in.) either end. This makes 'starting' the pins easier. Points should not yet protrude through inside of wood.

(c) Spread adhesive on section of each piece that will actually make contact with board.

(d) Place each piece against board and hammer home panel pins. Hammer along horizontal trajectory, pressing frame and board downwards to ensure flush finish at rear.

(e) Further support corners by hammering two panel pins, one through each piece. Hammer vertically to obtain tight fit (figure 29).

If it is decided to frame what we have earlier described as temporary or experimental work carried out on cardboard or hardboard, a simple way of framing is to glue the picture on to a second piece of hardboard (or plyboard) leaving a margin round the edges of this second piece. This margin should be equal to the thickness of the frame, which can be cut as before and fixed by a combination of adhesive and panel pins from the rear rather than from the side.

Four · Papier mâché masks

30

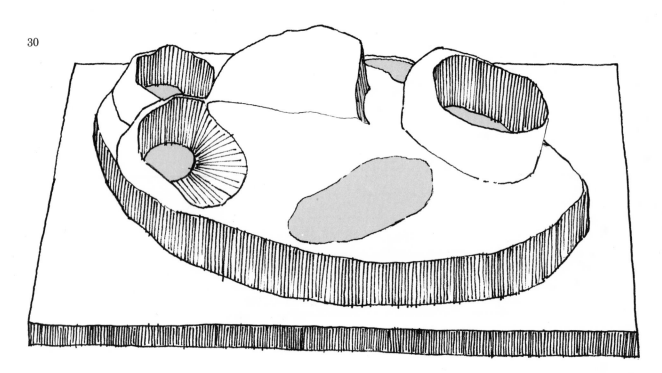

Materials

Clay or plasticine	Newspaper
Board	Newsprint
Petroleum jelly	Cellulose (wallpaper) paste
Glue brush	

Method

Shape head from clay or plasticine on board. Make sure thickness of head is at least 19 mm ($\frac{3}{4}$ in.) before features are added.

Add features, exaggerating shape and size (figure 30).

Cover with petroleum jelly.

Cover head with pieces of torn, *not cut,* newspaper, no larger than average postage stamp size. These should extend down sides to base.

Coat pieces well with paste. See that no edges stick up to spoil shape.

Repeat, using newsprint. (By alternating paper with print, one can see when each layer is complete).

Repeat layering process until mask has been coated six times in all.

Leave mask in warm place to dry (minimum 48 hours).

Remove clay or plasticine from the by now firm paper.

The papier mâché mask is more easily removed if previously applied to moist clay as, whilst drying, the clay shrinks and pulls itself away from inside of the mask.

Coat mask with seeds, using adhesive in normal manner.

Raffia was added for the hair on the masks in figure 50.

Five   Mobiles

31

32

Materials

Cotton

Wire

25 mm (1 in.) nail

Number of cardboard tubes,
various lengths

Hammer

Pliers

Battening (thin wood strips)
or dowelling

Method

Make two holes opposite each other 25 mm (1 in.) from top of each tube.

Cut each piece of wire 25 mm (1 in.) longer than diameter of tube (allowing 13 mm ($\frac{1}{2}$ in) for bending into shape shown in figure 31, and leaving 6 mm ($\frac{1}{4}$ in.) spare at each end).

Push wire through holes and keep in place by twisting ends with pliers.

Work mobile in as few seed types as possible, achieving contrast and simple design to show from distance.

Apply varnish.

Nail two pieces of battening, about 254 mm (10 in.) long, as shown in figure 32, bending nail to hold pieces together.

Attach cotton from bent wire inside tubes to battens, adjusting length to give desired hanging position. Balance tubes in pairs on opposite spokes of battens (see figure 99).

Six   Children's work

We have found that children from the age of four enjoy working with seeds, though where the very youngest are concerned the individual supervision required probably precludes attempting the work with more than a few children at a time.

Children will prefer to make a picture after only brief experimentation, and soon discover that seeds are quite suitable for making outlines. In fact, all the illustrations in this chapter show the very earliest attempts in the medium by children of widely differing ages and abilities. Figures 33 to 35 were made by young children within an hour and a half of their introduction to the medium. The pictures were developed by the children first drawing the outlines in pencil and then covering these outlines with seeds of their own choice. It is significant that they have chosen seeds to suit their purpose – Lee, the younger child, selecting larger seeds because they are easier to handle, making a bold outline, and Dany choosing smaller seeds to create a more delicate picture.

In figure 36 Alison wanted to use something else with the seeds, so chose brightly-coloured sticky paper which she cut into sympathetic shapes, alternating them with the seeds in a striped design.

The desire to fill in between the drawn outline to make a complete subject is apparent in figure 37, where more detail is included than in

33 and 34   Lee Morris aged 4

the previous work by younger children. Here, Stephen has tried to recreate exactly the facial characteristics of his parents, paying particular attention to the eyes, lips and hair.

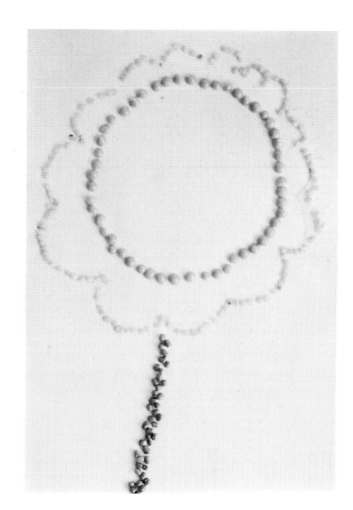

35 Dany Morris aged 5
36 Alison Batham aged 7

43

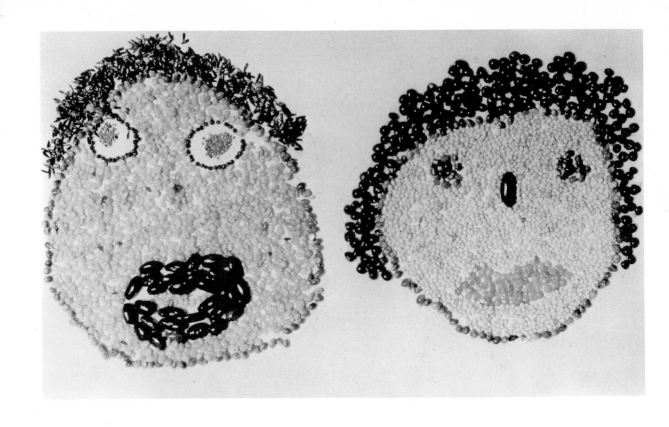

37 and 38   Stephen Manton aged 7

PLATE 2   Panels worked by a group of four 12 year olds. See page 46

38

To this point children had been given white cardboard on which to work, as it provides not only a good contrast with the seeds but also a clear ground on which to draw an outline. It was therefore a significant development when Stephen decided that the cat in figure 38 should not be allowed to sit on a white rug, and so chose grey cardboard instead. Although he did not work the background with seeds, he showed awareness of not only the subject, which has been the sole concern in all the illustrations so far in this chapter, but also of its surroundings.

For figure 38 a simple pencilled outline was drawn, but instead of working this outline with seeds Stephen decided that the body of his cat would be striped. He thought of using rows of seeds to represent the stripes without having drawn them first. When he had placed six rows he repeated the pattern. He deliberately left the head plain as he felt that stripes would obscure the details of the eyes and mouth. The whiskers were cut from white cord and added later.

The children who worked on the panels in figure 39 (see also plate 2) had previously experimented with basic design in a paper mosaic mural. For working with seeds they were given the theme of circles and ten seed types from which to choose. From thence they worked individually on ideas for a seed mural. The four shown here reveal a sympathy towards the seeds, bold use of the medium (so necessary in a mural) and a varied interpretation of the theme.

Two examples of formal pattern occur in figures 40 and 41. Elaine has most painstakingly carried out her rather ambitious and complicated design, using very small seeds. Colin's repeat pattern, although much simpler in concept, is equally effective.

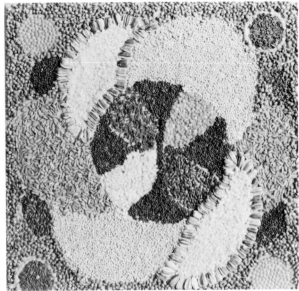

39 *Above left* Teresa Murphy, Joyce Logan, Michael Raymond, Christopher
Higgins aged 12 (see also Plate 2)

40 *Above right* Elaine Pullham aged 11

41 *Below* Colin Doyle aged 12

47

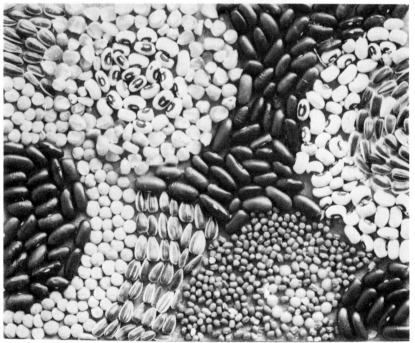

42 *Opposite above* Patrick Fields aged 12
43 *Opposite below* Phillip Noons aged 12
44 Tony Maher aged 13

Patrick and Phillip (figures 42 and 43) are concerned with the colour and texture of the seeds. Using a simple design to divide the board they filled in adjacent areas with seeds which were different in character and tone, achieving considerable movement and depth.

An increasing awareness of the use of a seed for a particular purpose, of design, of effectiveness of pattern and of subtlety of tone is apparent in figures 44-46 ,and these trends are continued in the final illustrations in this chapter. (For details of how to make masks such as those in figure 50 see page 39.)

45 Patrick Healey aged 13
46 Felicity Lambert, Julie Dainty, Sally O'Brien, Wanda Pogorzelski aged 13

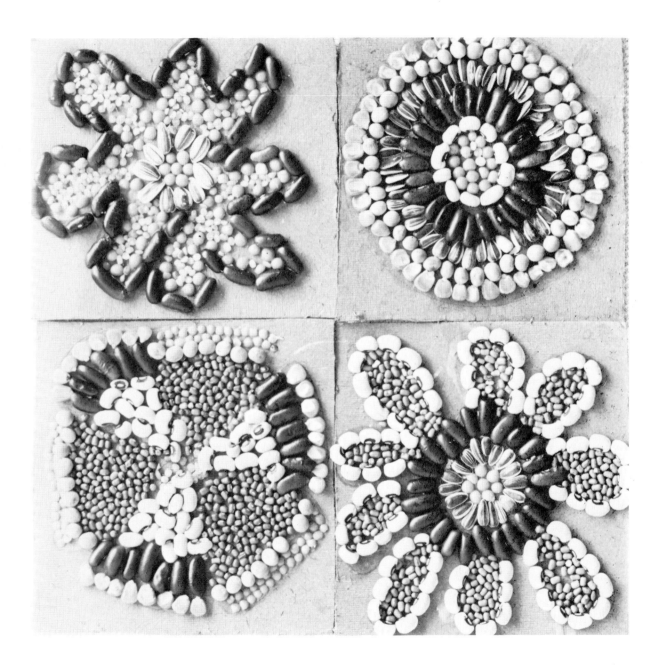

47   Kevin Blunt aged 14

48 Marie Lynsky aged 14

53

49 Pat Walker aged 14

50 Eugene Wooding, John Logan, Ronald Tarry, John Murray, David Murray aged 15

Children of all abilities are now able to extend their attention to detail to embrace work on a large scale. In general we would not recommend those under the age of thirteen to attempt a picture of greater dimensions than 305 mm × 305 mm (12 in. square), whether at home or in the classroom, because of the time and concentration needed, though it may be of interest to note that figures 51 and 52 were in fact submitted as course work for the Certificate of Secondary Education.

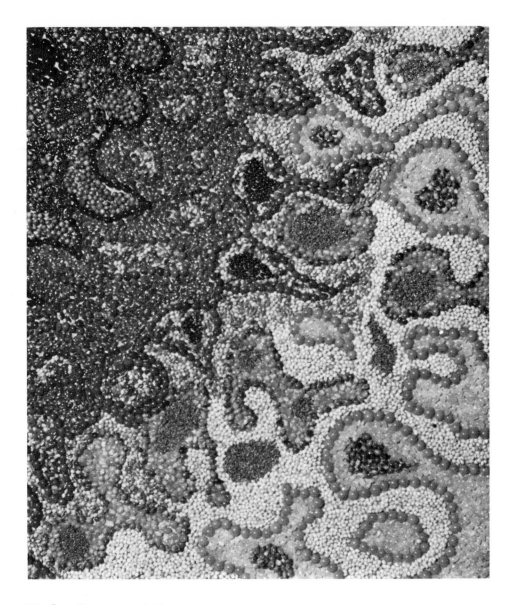

51 Jean Duncan aged 15

52   Linda Farrar aged 15

Seven   Creative techniques

Pattern

Some pictures may be comprised of one symmetrical pattern. Figure 90 was from its conception a design of this kind. Here it can be seen that large areas of one colour, not particularly interesting in themselves, can be used to create a satisfying balance. Strict adherence to line to achieve formal shapes is quite possible (see also figure 52) and, although working on designs like these is more mechanical than on pictures with smaller detailed areas, the results are rewarding enough to justify such an approach.

In considering the use of small patterned areas as part of a larger picture it is helpful to remember that often the most effective patterns are achieved with only a limited number of seed types (the 609 mm × 1219 mm (24 in. × 48 in.) *Singing Jaguar*, figure 93, employs only seven types). When working a pattern on a large picture one must be boldly decisive. The central herringbone pattern, seen in detail in figure 53, on the same picture is not a realistic representation of fur, but it is lavishly decorative in accordance with the over-all style of the picture. The sun-flower seeds suggest the texture and colour of fur, while the dwarf french beans provide a contrast which adds strength and direction to the creature itself. At the end of this upward sweep is another patterned

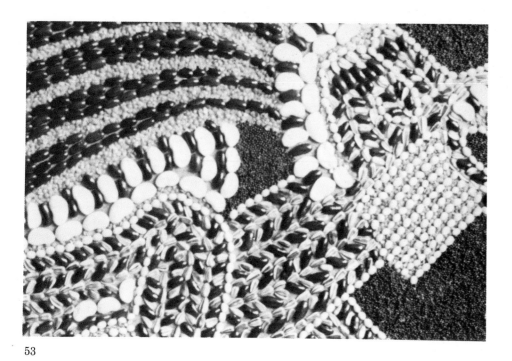

53

area, representing the gills. The direction is continued from the first pattern, but this time a simpler texture is created to suggest the folds of skin. The presence of haricot beans, to give height, and lentils, provides variance without ruining the continuity of the form of the animal. It is of note that the two examples described here, like the other two in the same section – the mane and the backbone – consist only of two seed types each.

While pattern is evident in many of the illustrations, one of the most interesting techniques has been to take one or two basic shapes and repeat them, slightly shifting the emphasis each time (see figures 55, 91, 96, 97 and 98).

54

Relief

There is considerable opportunity to achieve relief in work with seeds, as the heights of seed types vary a great deal. Butter beans with a background of rape seed, as used in figure 53, enable the subject to stand out quite markedly. Relief can play an important part in the presentation of the subject itself. In figure 91 the pink lentils are set into the higher circles of split peas. This example is more subtle than the first, for both seeds are circular, but with the shadow thrown by the split peas and the fact that the lentils are smaller, the inner circle appears to recede.

Another way of achieving relief may be seen in figures 54 (detail of figure 97) and 95, where seeds have been built up in layers in order to highlight certain features.

55

Texture, contrast and colour

Some seeds, although having a smooth surface, possess distinctive markings which can give the impression of texture. Perhaps the best example is the sunflower seed. In figure 95 the effect of twigs, sticks and stalks is suggested by the tonal stripes of the sunflower seeds which also assist the simulation of the woven composition of the real object. The softer interior of the nest is achieved with lighter melon (honeydew) seeds, presenting a lining sympathetic to the nest itself. Again, in figure 62 (see also Plate 3), the variety of the individual stones is recreated, producing not only the differences in colour and shape, but also the rough and smooth surfaces. In this picture both the gunga beans and the sunflower seeds have been sorted to present uniformly lighter and darker areas.

Colour contrasts are most important, and work with seeds is not limited to the obvious use of light and dark, though the effect of this fundamental balance may be seen in particular in figures 56, 57, 93 and 96. One can also achieve subtle colour distinctions, as in figure 91, where the proximity of the orange split peas to the pink lentils adds vibrance, as opposed to the more obviously contrasted areas of the picture, and in figure 55, where the alternation of the two large areas of brown seeds gives, through their relationship to the predominantly white ground and their own interplay, an added dimensional quality.

Effect of line

When working with seeds for the first time (particularly with children) the best way to become familiar with the qualities of the seeds is to use them in a linear manner, creating the external boundaries of the subject. Later, line may play a prominent role in more ambitious work, and often the initial design will reveal a predominantly linear subject. In figures 56 and 98 the essential structure is linear, and the direction and development of these lines has had to be evolved with particular care. The infilling between the lines adds a lacy softness.

56

Incorporating ground into design

Colours additional to those of seeds may be obtained by painting the background of the picture before the seeds are placed. Even where it is the intention to cover the ground with seeds, there will inevitably be many gaps according to the shapes and sizes of the seeds used. In figure 62 (see also Plate 3) the white ground showing irregularly through the dark seeds emphasises the mottled appearance already noted. The earlier observations on design and the shape of the board are especially relevant when using a painted ground which is to be an integral part of the whole picture. For single colour grounds (see figure 56) all areas of the picture should present a balance between ground and seeds rather than having an area of seeds surrounded by an empty expanse of ground.

An entirely new area of experimentation is opened up if two or more colours are used for painted grounds. Here the ground immediately assumes more importance than before, whilst the role of the seeds is also altered. The painted ground could also be used in conjunction with fabric and paper, or substituted by them.

Translucency

Rice is the most translucent grain we have found. This grain takes on the hue of the ground used, as in figure 56, where the rice adopts a mauve tint from the purple paint. In figure 57 white paint was applied to the area on which the rice was to be used, effecting a whiter and more opaque appearance than would normally have resulted.

57

58

Mixing

Mixing types of seeds can produce a variety of effects. One of the most interesting of these is the gradual tonal change which would be impossible with most types of seed alone. The use of this technique may be seen in figure 58, in which the elephant has a roundness of form in marked contrast to the relatively flat areas around it. For the deeper tones on the body brown lentils alone were used. Lighter pearl barley was introduced in increasing quantities in proportion to the amount of light required, until the darker seeds were omitted altogether. This blend was particularly successful as both types of seed were of similar shape and size.

In figure 98 this device is taken further, as three seeds are mixed together; rice, pearl barley and yellow lentils. The effect of this is heightened by the circles of sunflower seeds which themselves add a complementary tonal value. Again, the tonal area is offset by the adjacent flat area.

Colour and type of seed for subject
Care must be taken to select the most appropriate seeds for the work in hand. Much will depend, of course, on the variety of seeds available as well as on the individual peculiarities of the seed types. Assuming that a reasonable range of seeds has been collected, the following examples of selection may be useful.

When working fine detail small seeds must be used. In figure 59, which is a detail from figure 89, the area shown measures an actual 203 mm × 279 mm (8 in. × 11 in.). The features of the faces have been described in red rape seed, while in order to capture the delicacy of the original work the entire picture has been built up with no seed larger than the split pea. The first detail from this picture (figure 58) again demonstrates the minute working necessitated by the subject.

By way of contrast the strong backbone of the *Singing Jaguar* (figure 93) is ably suggested by the heavy, smooth butter beans, as are the pillars at the edges of the picture.

Figure 27 (see also Plate 1), influenced by mould formed on home-made wine, is another example of careful selection. The periphery of dried peas and haricot beans is higher than the centre of the picture and gives one the impression of looking down into the flagon. The background of red rape seed implies the colour of wine, on which float the furry congestions of the mould itself, recreated by various combinations of seed types.

59

69

Eight   Subject sources

The importance of careful subject selection has already been mentioned. This chapter may suggest a number of sources particularly suited to seed collage. Any art form relies on visual experience for its creation and understanding. Learning to look at even quite ordinary objects can produce fascinating study. Recognition of the inexhaustible supply of visual material which is at hand is all that is needed—tree bark, caterpillars on leaves, the fur of animals, bales of straw, opaque glass, tile patterns, chimney-stacks, piles of bricks and heaps of sacks are but a few random examples of the wealth of shapes, tonal areas and designs around us. The problem soon becomes not the search for a suitable subject but the selection of just one from the many.

Even as experience increases and more diverse or demanding pictures are undertaken there is no necessity to seek more sophisticated subject-matter. The challenge may well lie in one's definition of a subject. A developing interpretation of the same subject may be witnessed in the series based on cell structures, where figures 97 and 98 have evolved from figures 81 and 91.

The art forms of primitive and ancient civilisations are readily translated into this medium by virtue of their basic colour and highly decorative qualities—features which are often prominent in the pictures illustrated in this book. Figures 55, 89, 93 and 96 are examples of interpretations taken from such sources.

However, it would be wrong to indicate that decorative work, although seeds are ideally suited to it, should be the only approach to, or end-product of, the medium. As discussed in the previous chapter depth, shadow, contrast between light and dark tones and three-dimensional effects can all be obtained, though as much care must be taken in planning and execution when developing such techniques as in other types of seed collage.

60   Stone from which figure 57 was taken

61

62 *Pebbles*   609 mm × 609 mm (24 in. × 24 in.)
A bold interpretation of the shapes and markings of specially grouped stones from
the beach. A painted white ground assists in creating a mottled effect (see also
Plate 3)

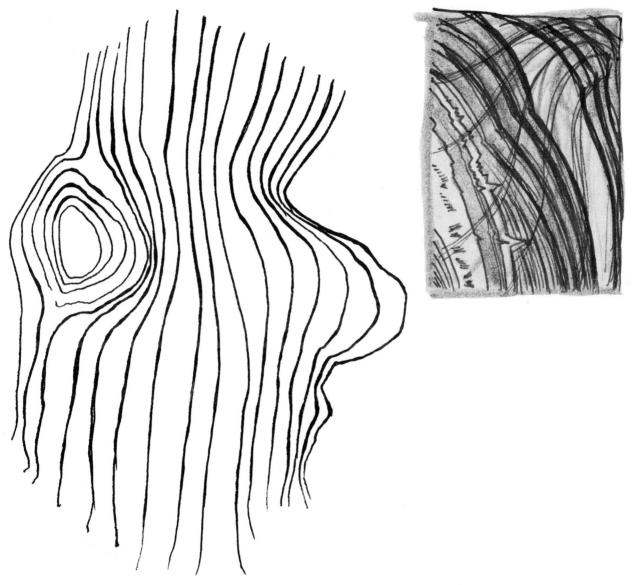

63 and 64   Drawings of contours and saw-cuts of wood

73

66

65 Original drawing for works shown in figures 106 and 107

67 *Opposite   Ophelia*   686 mm × 433 mm (27 in. × 21 in.)
Very few of the seeds here are smooth or shiny, so that the textural surface alludes to
the wood grain which suggested the picture (see figure 66). In soft beige and greys
with blue shading

74

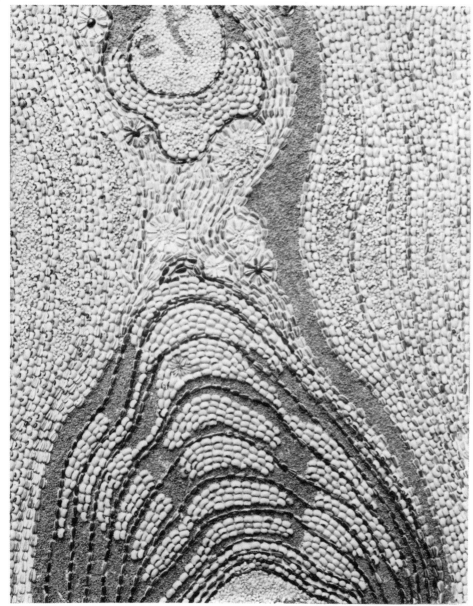

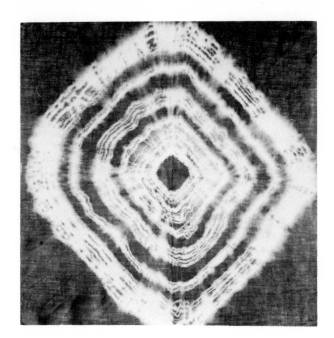
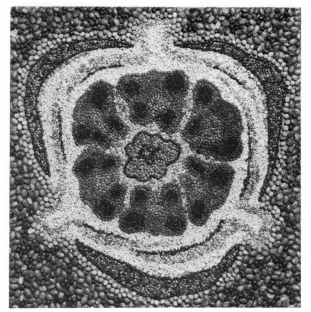

68 Tie-dyed fabric suggests a variety of natural forms
69 Cross-section of a flower bud by Linda Farrar

PLATE 3 3a *Pebbles* 609 mm × 609 mm (24 in. × 24 in.)
A bold interpretation of the shapes and markings of specially grouped stones from
the beach
3b *Tree* 457 mm × 457 mm (18 in. × 18 in.)
A free interpretation of slender, arched branches using only four types of seed

70 to 75   Ideas for seed pictures may be evolved from simple stimuli

77

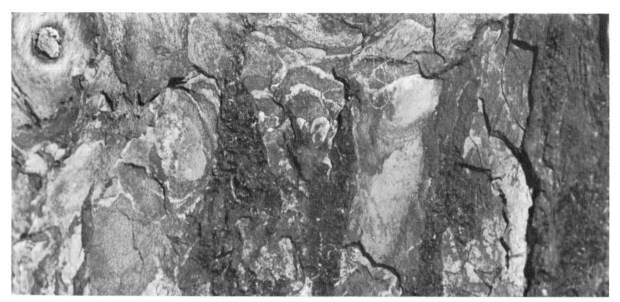

76

The piece of wood pictured in figure 66 also possessed an evocative bark covering
(see figure 76) suggesting wings. This idea was elaborated upon to include a variety
of patterns, all depicted in browns and greens. The drawings show the simplification
of the original idea before the picture (figure 80) was attempted.

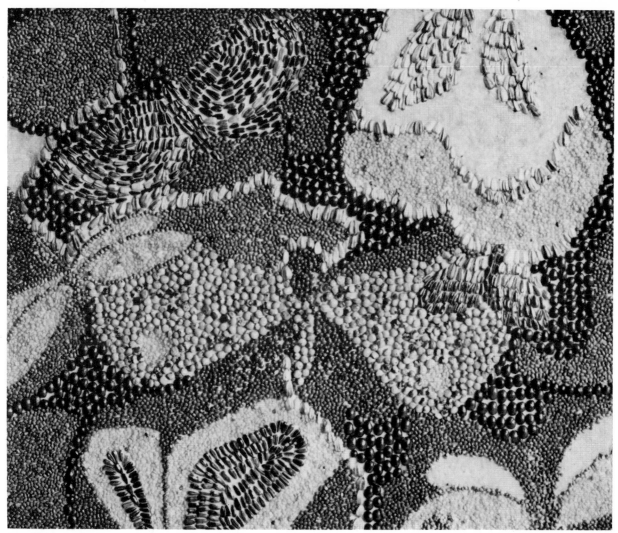

80   *Moths*   457 mm × 609 mm (18 in. × 24 in.)

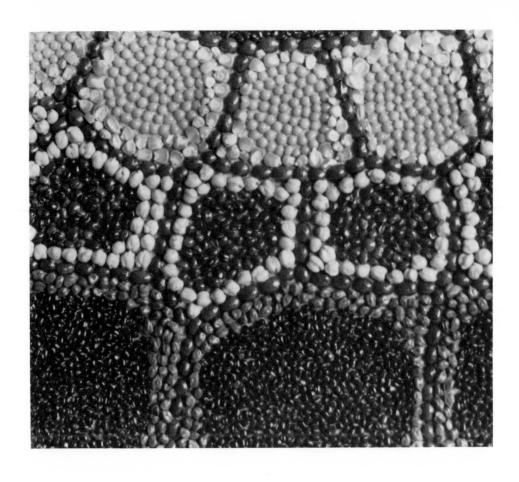

81 *Cell Structure II*   229 mm × 305 mm (9 in. × 12 in.)
One of a series on this theme, coloured in rich brown and yellow

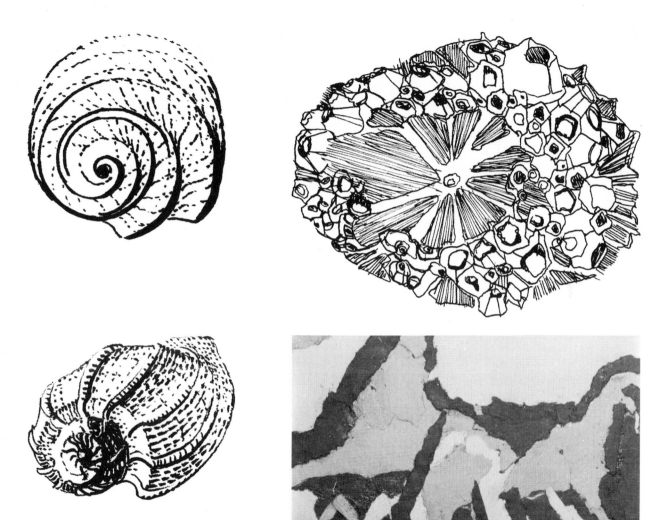

82 to 85   Further interesting ideas may be suggested by shells

86

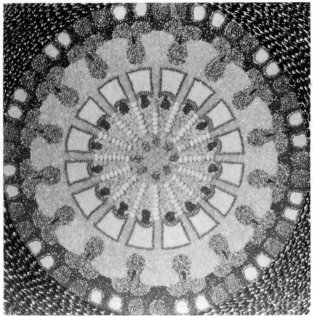

87 *Sea Urchin*   609 mm × 609 mm (24 in. × 24 in.)
In this cross-section Jean Duncan has used rich shades of crimson, yellow and white
to achieve a pleasing balance

88   *Reflection*   457 mm × 609 mm (18 in. × 24 in.)
Suggested by the shapes of meat carcasses hanging in a shop window

89 *Opposite Procession* 918 mm × 609 mm (36 in. × 24 in.)
Taken from an eighteenth-century Indian wall-painting but with several figures
omitted to avoid complication. Care was taken to preserve the same balance of colour
values as existed in the original. The curves on the painting lent themselves to fluent
expression in seeds.

90 *Solar* 609 mm × 609 mm (24 in. × 24 in.)
A simple yet serene pattern in which the seeds have coped with exacting curves

87

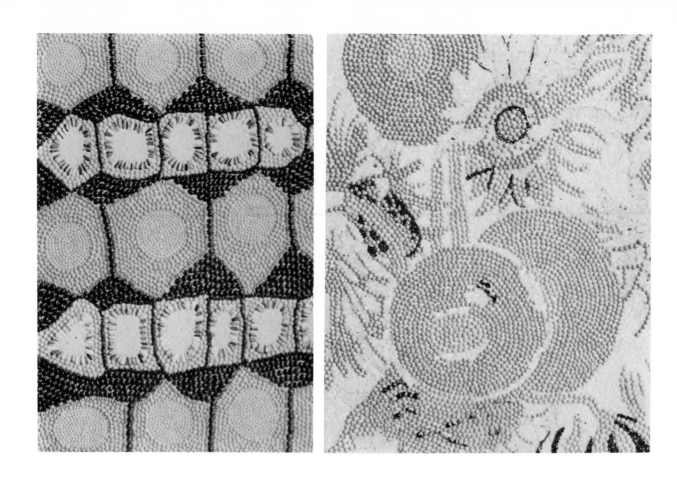

91 *Cell Structure I* 609 mm × 609 mm (24 in. × 24 in.) Detail
The vibrant pink and orange circles give an optical effect which is accentuated by the recession of the centres

92 *Sunflowers* 609 mm × 609 mm (24 in. × 24 in.) Detail
A delicate reconstruction of Van Gogh's masterpiece carried out in white, yellow and gold

93 *Singing Jaguar* 609 mm × 1219 mm (24 in. × 48 in.)
Based on an ancient Mexican religious symbol, this vigorous design is achieved by
the use of a few, well-chosen seeds

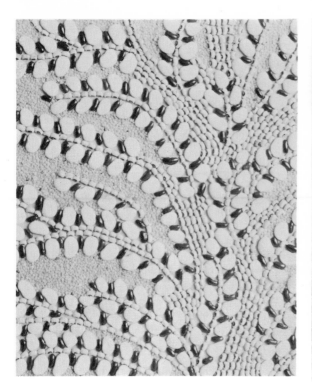 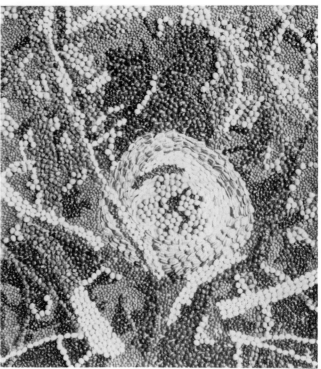

94 *Tree* 457 mm × 457 mm (18 in. × 18 in.) Detail
This free interpretation of slender, arched branches uses only four seed types (see also Plate 4)

95 *Nest* 457 mm × 407 mm (18 in. × 16 in.)
The effect of the mossy tangle of leaves, twigs and straw in natural colours has preserved a feeling of depth

96 *Opposite* *Design I* 609 mm × 584 mm (24 in. × 23 in.)
The first of two pictures taken from modern Aboriginal paintings. A sense of movement is suggested by the interplay between the dark brown, yellow and white areas

91

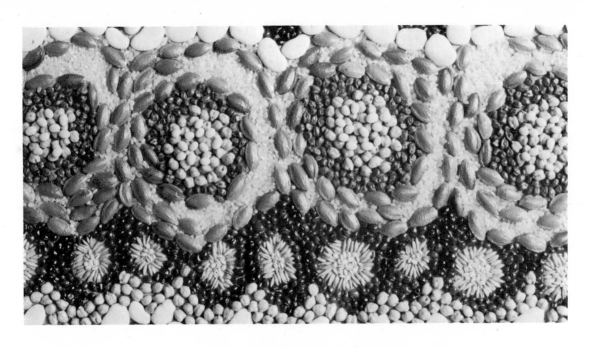

97 *Autumn* 305 mm × 432 mm (12 in. × 17 in.)
Using rich browns this highly-textured study catches autumnal tones in flowing
movement

PLATE 4 *Trees* 766 mm × 609 mm (30 in. × 24 in.)
See figures 65, 106 and 107

98 *Cobweb* 457 mm × 457 mm (18 in. × 18 in.)
The strong structure does not detract from the lacy impression of yellows and
whites

93

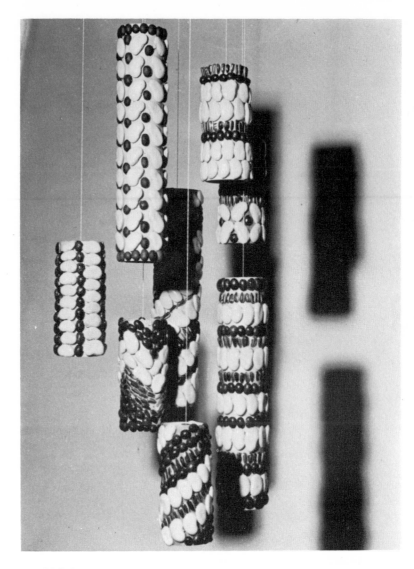

99 *Mobile*
Here three seed types only are arranged in formal patterns. As the cylinders spin the designs combine to suggest more complicated structures

100   *Tawny Owls*   508 mm × 305 mm (20 in. × 12 in.)
A formal but dramatic posing of the rufous and tawny phases of these birds. A
simplified but integrated combination of seeds implies the markings of wing bars and
tail feathers

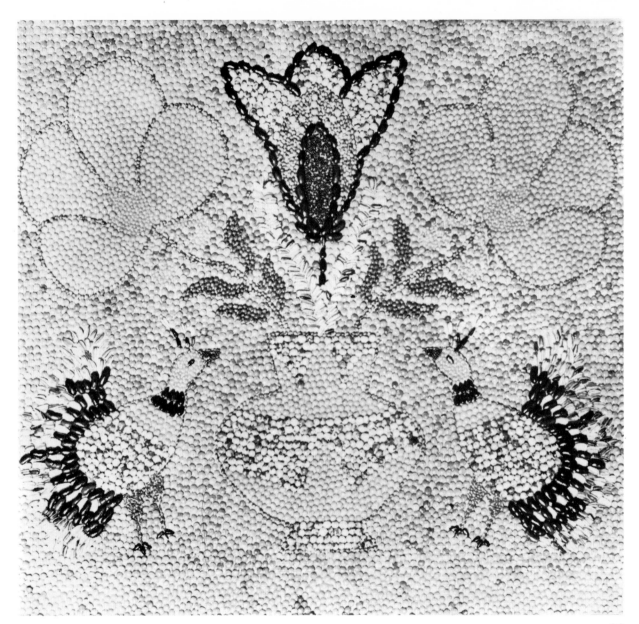

101 *Opposite Peacocks* 609 mm × 609 mm (24 in. × 24 in.)
This highly decorative work by Margaret Micklethwaite was suggested by Hungarian embroidery. The khaki ground supports predominantly yellow figures

102 *Garland* 609 mm × 457 mm (24 in. × 18 in.)
Margaret Micklethwaite has added an interesting speckled ground to give freedom to an otherwise formal flower design

97

103 *Birth of a Flower*   609 mm × 609 mm (24 in. × 24 in.)
In this absorbing treatment of the subject, full of swirling movement, Jean Duncan
has offset the hard edges by soft, smokey hollyhock seeds

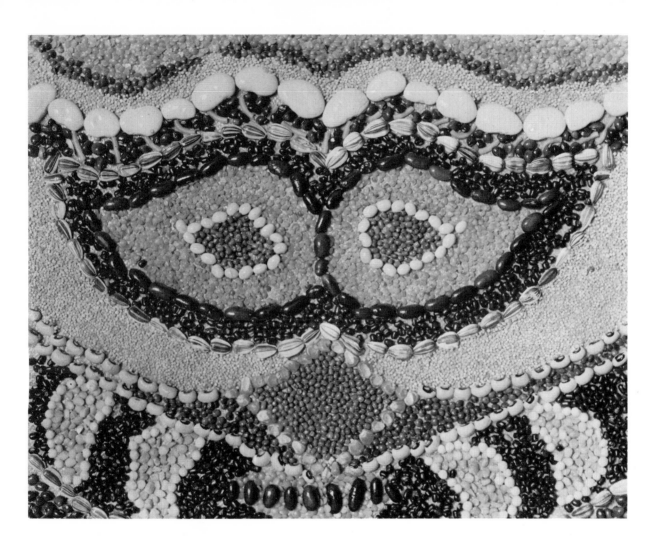

104   *Mask*   305 mm × 356 mm (12 in. × 14 in.)
Use of many seed types has made this mask by Evelyn Morris vivid and colourful

99

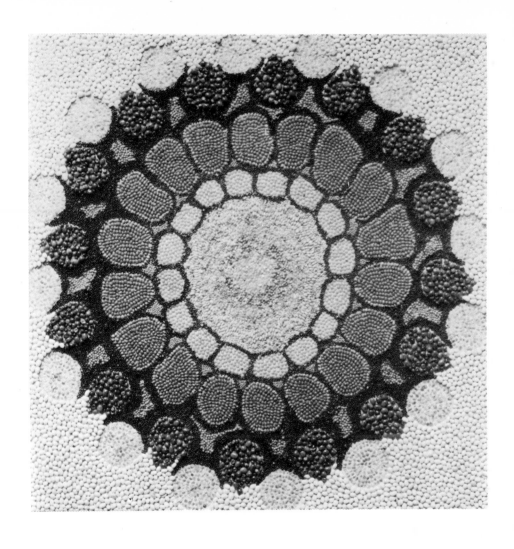

105 *Corolla* 609 mm × 609 mm (24 in. × 24 in.)
Linda Farrar has used the height of the seeds to project the outer edges of her picture forwards, while the vibrant yellowish centre recedes because of the linear use of black rape seed

106 Carmel Cauchi adapted this painting for the picture which follows

107 *Trees* 766 mm × 609 mm (30 in. × 24 in.)
The sweep in the curves of the trees and the three-dimensional effect assist Carmel
Cauchi's dramatic composition (see also Plate 4)

Seed chart

BASIC COLOUR	LARGE	MEDIUM	SMALL	TINY
White	Butter bean	White bean Haricot bean Black-eye bean Melon (honeydew) Orange pip Sunflower†	Polished rice White dari	
Beige		Chick pea	Pearl barley Patna rice (long grained) Clipped oat	Plate millet Pannicum millet Grass Mazagan canary
Yellow			Yellow lentil	
Orange		Split pea Maize (Indian corn)	Wheat	Mustard
Red	Runner bean* (Stringbean) Broad bean*	Dwarf french bean	Milo Red lentil	Red rape seed
Light brown			Parsnip White peppercorn	
Mid brown	Plum stone	Maple pea Tickbean Gunga bean* Rose cacao bean*	Casha Hollyhock Red lentil (outer)	Teazle Linseed Whole cummin
Dark brown		Coffee bean Cowpea Pimento Apple pip		
Green	Pumpkin	Dried pea Continental lentil	Yellow lentil (outer)	
Blue				Maw (poppy seed)
Grey		Sunflower†	Hemp (unobtain- able in USA)	
Black		Sunflower†	Tare Black peppercorn	Niger (Rantil) Black rape seed

*darker speckles   † also with stripes of mid and dark brown

Suppliers

Acrylic paints and co-polymer emulsion paints

Clifford Milburn Limited
54 Fleet Street, London, E C 4

George Rowney and Company
10-11 Percy Street, London W 1

Reeves and Sons Limited
Lincoln Road, Enfield, Middlesex

Stafford-Reeves Incorporated
626 Greenwich Street, New York, N Y 10014, U S A

The Morilla Company Incorporated
43-01 21st Street, Long Island City, New York, U S A

The Morilla Company of California
2866 West Seventh Street, Los Angeles, California, U S A

Adhesives

Evostick Resin 'W'
Most stationers and general stores

Dufix
W H Smith, art stores

Marvin Medium
Margros Limited
Monument House, Monument Way West, Woking, Surrey

Eagle Pencil Company
Danbury, Connecticut, U S A

Elmer's Glue and *Sobo*
Hardware stores, most general stores and builders' supply houses

Varnishes

Marine and artists' suppliers

General Supplier

Large variety of useful supplies and equipment available from:
Art & Crafts Unlimited
49 Shelton Street, London W C 2